The Insightful Journey:

Guided Journal

Terry Dubroy and Jillian-Rae Picco

ISBN: 978-1-7389779-3-2

First published in 2023 by Thrive: Enabling Potential.

www.enablingpotential.ca

This Journey Belongs To:

____

Introduction

When we read books, we absorb information; when we reflect on what we read, we solidify our understanding so that we can take mindful action. The reflective writing prompts in this guided journal will enable you to understand yourself, to deepen a connection with your authentic self, and feel empowered to continue practising balance in your life.

Each chapter within this journal expands on the wisdom provided in *The Insightful Journey*. Similarly to the way that we encouraged you to approach reading the book, we now invite you to notice the chapters that best resonate with your personal growth. You do not have to follow this book in a linear way. The prompts within each chapter are designed to support you no matter where you currently find yourself in life, so you can always leave certain chapters blank and return to them if you need them in the future. You can start with A and work your whole way through to Z. You can start with S, then go to L, then go to Q and J and E. There are no steadfast rules to follow, as this is a self-reflective adventure worthy of your curious wanderings.

Thank you for choosing to take another step to walk the High Road in your life – to take it one letter, one moment, one day at a time.

The Toolkit

This 'Toolkit' suggests the times in your life that you may be struggling with a specific issue, and benefit from doing some 'inner work' related to the chapter that corresponds for your growth and healing. Whether you are experiencing one of the valleys of your journey or climbing towards the peaks, you can return here for lighthearted guidance.

Affirmations – 4

A tool for reassuring and embracing your authentic self.

Believe in Yourself – 8

A tool for reflecting on and updating your goals and dreams.

Change – 12

A tool for the moments where you know you need to make shifts in your life, whether small or large, and it is overwhelming.

Doing – 18

A tool for when you are stuck in thinking or feeling mode, when you have been overdoing it to the point of burnout, or going a bit overboard in the reckless behaviour department.

Egolessness – 22

A tool for grounding your spirit when your ego is causing you to act out of character.

Faith in Yourself – 28

A tool for the moments when it feels like no one in your life has faith in you, and then you remember that it is okay because there is a tool for that.

Greatness – 32

A tool for motivating yourself when it feels like you have been experiencing a plateau in your life for a bit too long.

Happiness – 36

A tool you need when you are beginning to think that happiness is fleeting; maybe something that temporarily made you happy is gone.

Inspire – 40

A tool for when you are lacking energy or feeling uninspired.

Just 'Be' – 44

A tool for when you feel constantly drained, especially by the noise of society, other people, or the external world in general.

Value – 100

A tool for when you realise that you want to distance yourself from what you know in your gut is not adding value to your life.

Withitness – 104

A tool for when you need a grounding perspective, an inspirational reminder of why what you do feeds into the greater picture.

X Marks Your Spot – 108

A tool that serves as a reminder of the potential that there is for you right now.

Yes to Life – 114

A tool for when you are on the fence, teeter-tottering unsteadily out of fear of the unknown.

Zeroes Are No Longer Permitted – 118

A tool that will always remind you to be grateful of how far you have come, and how far you will continue to go.

Welcome to the High Road –

to *your* insightful journey.

Layer One: Self-acceptance

When you accept yourself, you can accept your reality for what it is.

"What is the hidden, yet authentic version of yourself deprived of? Perhaps your heart is calling you to move your life in a different direction that is more aligned with what works best for you."

A

Affirmations

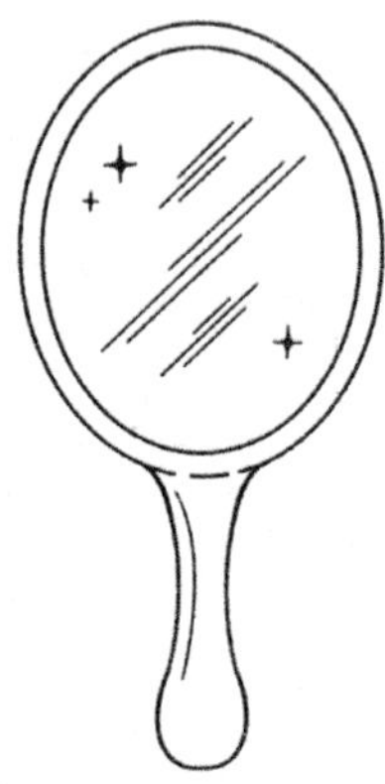

Affirmative Self-love

It is very normal for us to struggle with self-esteem, self-love, and self-confidence throughout our lives. Whether we experience these difficulties internally or as a result of messages that others project onto us, choosing affirmations allows us to remember the better version of ourselves. You can think of affirmations as being like an 'inner mirror' that helps you to remember your goals, what your values are, and how you are working towards believing in yourself. Giving yourself an affirmation is like giving yourself the ultimate reminder: that you already have what you need within to thrive.

My Prompts for Affirmations

What is one area of my life that I feel unsteady in? Is there an affirmation that can reassure me through this?

What way of giving myself an affirmation speaks to me? Would I like to begin writing down an affirmation every morning, for instance, or to speak to myself in the mirror?

What are some other kind affirmations that I could say to myself? I can brainstorm them here. If it is difficult to think of anything positive, I can think about what I would say to someone I fully loved, knowing that this is what I am working towards.

B
Believe

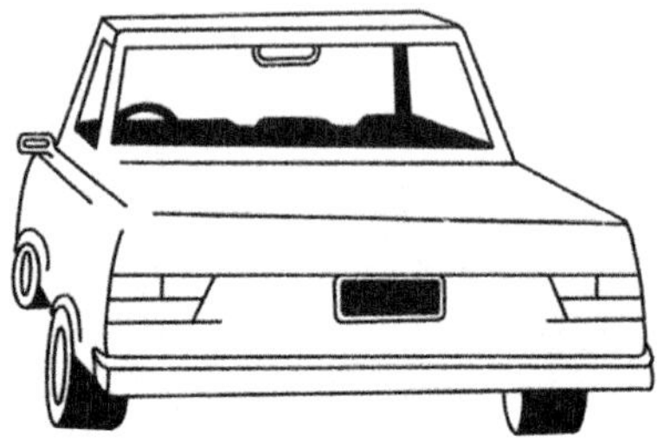

You Are Worth Believing In

You are worth believing in. While the truth of this cannot be understated, the reality is that to truly believe in yourself, you need a foundation made of long, mid, and short-term goals. Long-term goals relate to your utmost dreams and visions in life, and because they are a product of your spirit and imagination, you do not have to limit yourself to dreaming small. You never know what can happen. If your long-term vision feels a bit foggy, try thinking about one of your natural strengths, or something that you loved to do when you were young. Remember, the reason it is best to begin by reflecting on long-term visions is because from that point you can break your bigger dreams down into smaller steps, such as attainable mid-term (about 6 months) and short-term goals (ones that can occur on a daily basis).

My Prompts for Believing

Long-term goals – Do I have any ideas related to my long-term vision? What might it look like if I succeeded as a result of having practised one of my gifts or interests consistently in the long-term?

Mid-term goals – What are some objectives that I can set to accomplish within the next six months – in two seasons from now?

Short-term goals – What do I need to accomplish on a daily, weekly, and monthly basis to make my mid-term objectives a reality? How can I make these goals obtainable for myself?

C

Change

Unfolding Into Change

Change is a natural part of life, yet often a part of life that many of us learn to resist. A major part of your self-love journey lies in understanding that self-acceptance is not an excuse to accept yourself as you are, because the condition of growth relates to making positive changes in mind, body, and spirit. Be gentle with yourself and begin by making a small, attainable change. Focus on what is a priority for you right now – focus on making a change in the area that you feel the most unbalanced. If you feel unbalanced in your mind, reflect on a recurring negative thought you have and how you could reframe it. If you feel unbalanced in your body, think about how you could make more time in your life to exercise, get fresh air, or try a new, healthier recipe. For your spirit – well, your heart knows. Let your heart spill out in these pages if you feel that you are in need of connecting with your spirituality or emotions.

My Prompts for Change

Which aspect of making changes in my life (mind, body, or spirit)
resonated with me when I read this chapter?

How could I negotiate with myself to welcome a different, yet beneficial state of being in this (or these) area(s)? Perhaps I could set an attainable short-term goal related to these changes.

When I think about a change within myself unfolding, what does that look like in the long-term? Does it relate to internal shifts (my inner world's perceptions), and/or external shifts (something I begin to do)?

Layer Two: Taking Action

When you choose mindful actions, you will not question whether you are going in the right direction.

"Whether you are 16 or 60, the experiences that you subject yourself to beyond your comfort zone define the extent to which you will grow... character is built when our actions move us from our comfort zone to learning zones."

– The Insightful Journey

D

Doing

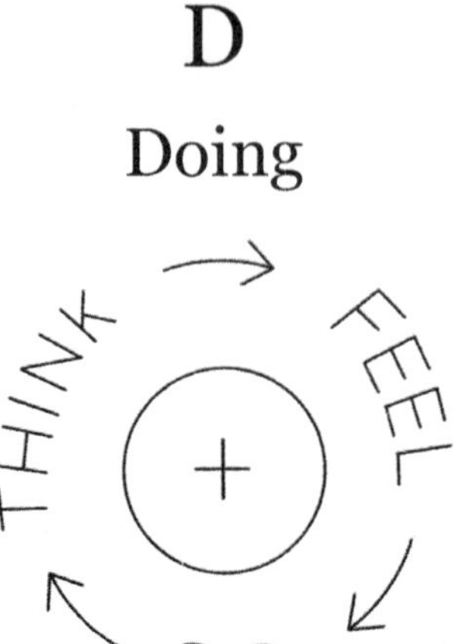

Becoming a Mindful Doer

Predominant thinkers are inclined to spend most of their time in their heads; predominant feelers are inclined to spend most of their time in their emotions; predominant doers are inclined to spend most of their time in constant, busy-bee action. Yet balance is about following all three of these in order to take action: thinking mindfully first, immersing yourself in impactful or even spiritual feelings related to the meaning of what you are going to do, and then taking intentional action. When you practise these three steps, making the extra effort to go into the areas you are less comfortable in, you will step out of your 'comfort zone' and into your 'learning zone'. In your learning zones, the greatest adventures of your life will occur, as you will build the most self-confidence and have the most intentional experiences. Ultimately, cycling through this three-step process on a daily basis will lead you to actions that enable you to love yourself and love your life.

My Prompts for Mindful Doing

Do I consider myself to be a predominant thinker, feeler, or doer? How has my predominant tendency proved to be a strength throughout my life?

Are there any steps I can take to challenge my comfort zone in the other two areas of mindful doing that I am less familiar with?

Can I think of any ways that I want to challenge my comfort zone in general? When I look at my long-term goals, what new learning experiences do they call me out of my 'nest' to engage in?

E
Egolessness

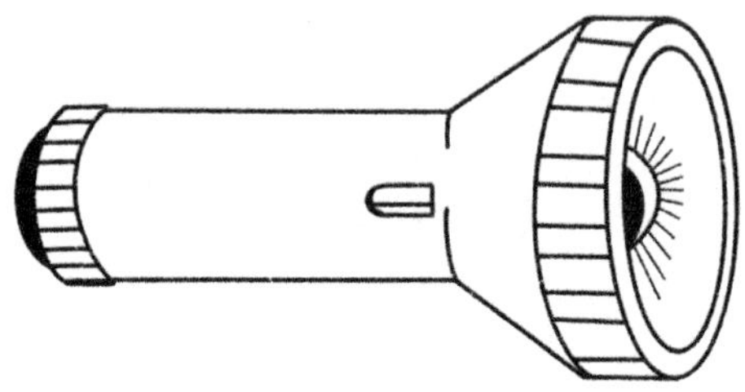

Levelling Your Ego

Our ego is our basic sense of self-worth. In today's society, many of us fall into extreme behaviours where our self-worth is either inflated (we think that we are superior to others because of ABC) or deflated (we think that we are inferior to others because of ABC). The reality is that we cannot love ourselves or other people with a superior or inferior sense of ego. When we live this way, we become disconnected from ourselves and the world around us, because we are either 'too high' or 'too low' to be balanced.

My Prompts for Egolessness

When does my ego tend to react the most? Does it put me on a pedestal (superiority), or cause me to hide my authentic self (inferiority)? Why do I think this is?

How does understanding how I struggle with my ego help me to accept where I am on my journey? How can I be gentle with myself while also being honest?

Am I ready to practise Egolessness? If so, how could I utilise one of the other tools in this guide (e.g. affirmations, deep breathing) to ground me when my ego is out of balance in the future?

Layer Three: Opening to Possibility

When you are open to possibility, you will be able to move away from the crowd when you need to create your own fulfilment.

"When you are not experiencing the weather of the day that you would like, what matters is finding meaning within it and being gentle with yourself. When the sun is not there, it is simply behind the clouds."

– *The Insightful Journey*

F

Faith in Yourself

When You Need Faith the Most

This chapter was especially important for the insights it shared on the concept of 'failing forward'. We all encounter failure in life, and the true test of having faith in ourselves is whether or not we allow these experiences to set us back, or move us forward. It is normal if you are hard on yourself when you experience 'failure', and in truth, you are probably hard on yourself because you care so much. You are probably doing better than you often realise, so there is no point in losing faith. Even when you do slip up, this reflection prompt now gives you the opportunity to notice in hindsight how all experiences of failure or faithlessness were important for your growth.

My Prompts for Having Faith in Myself

How do I tend to react when I make mistakes or encounter failure?

How could I focus on 'failing forward' and be gentle with myself when these situations arise?

What is a situation where I struggle to have faith in myself? How could I empower myself, utilising the key to faith by unlocking some of my potential for growth?

G

Greatness

The Journey of Your Greatness

The idea of Egolessness, that no one is better than anyone else, can be applied to Greatness. Sometimes our perception of Greatness can be that only the people we put on pedestals, perhaps watching on television or otherwise, are capable of accomplishing ultimate success. In reality, the short, mid, and long term goals you set in the Believe chapter, combined with your ability to apply the tools you need during challenging situations, is what will ultimately lead you to your personal Greatness. Your personal Greatness is about what originates from you and allows you to fully embody and practise the gifts that are innate within your authentic self. It is incredibly self-loving and powerful to make efforts to move towards this, even if what your Greatness fully looks like is still a mystery to you.

My Prompts for Greatness

What do the 'three peaks' of Greatness make me dream of (e.g. my accomplishments growing over time)?

What is unique and original about me? Do I make enough time in my life to be my own person and do what I am innately gifted at?

What is one step I could take this week (perhaps levelling up on one of my goals set in the Believe chapter) to build upon my strengths, moving from a plateau towards the next peak?

H
Happiness

The Truth About Happiness

There is a difference between 'sugar-rush happiness' and 'thriving happiness'. Unfortunately, narratives in society tend to push agendas of happiness that relate to the sugar-rush and temporary moments of bliss, rather than the truth of longlasting contentment. Giving yourself the opportunity to go inward now, and notice what truly allows you to feel balanced and loving towards yourself on a long-term, consistent basis, is where you will come to experience a deeper sense of fulfillment in life.

My Prompts for Happiness

What parts of my life currently bring me happiness? Is there something I have realised would make me even happier that I could do, especially as it relates to my strengths, interests, and three-part balance (mind, body, and spirit)?

Is there anything in my life that is making me unhappy? How could I stop pressing the 'repeat' button on this negativity?

When I think of my ideal future self, what have I surrounded myself with to create my own fulfilment?

I
Inspire

Creating Your Own Inspired Energy

In this chapter, we reflected on the idea of 'loving limits' and of creating spiritual clearings that enable an inspired, grateful state of being. 'Loving limits' relate to understanding that sometimes, from a caring place, we end up overextending and giving all of our energy to other people or circumstances. We feel depleted afterwards, and then we wonder why we do not feel inspired, giving, or grateful in life. We invite you to reflect on 'loving limits' you may need to set in your life so that you can maintain your clearing, and ensure that you are giving to the world 'from a full cup' rather than an empty one, so to speak.

My Prompts for Inspiration

What immediately comes to mind when I think about creating clarity within myself?

Are there any people or circumstances in my life that make me feel like I am being drained of inspiration? If so, could I set 'loving limits', perhaps spending less time and energy in these areas so that I am fulfilled?

What is inspiring me about my life right now? Do my inspirations
relate to my future? If I am not feeling inspired, what could I do to
gather inspiration?

J

Just 'Be'

Moderating Under and Overstimulation

A 'loudness' dial allows us to fine-tune how we interact with what we perceive as being too underwhelming or overwhelming in our lives. Depending on your personality, you will either find yourself frequently bored and restless, yet waiting on others to bring the fun to you, or you will find yourself overwhelmed and drained by factors in your environments that you feel you cannot control. Fine-tuning your loudness dial is about reflecting on how you can internally moderate your sense of being underwhelmed or overwhelmed, rather than allowing yourself to constantly be negatively impacted by external circumstances.

My Prompts for Just Being

What does the phrase 'just be' mean to me? What does it make me feel like doing, or even, like not doing?

Do I ever find that the 'noise of life' negatively impacts me? If so, what measures could I take to 'dial down' or 'dial up', to mediate with it rather than allowing it to upset me?

How do I envision my life improving when I become a master at 'just being'? How will I feel internally, and what will I be doing differently?

Layer Four: Perceiving Life Differently

When you perceive life differently, the negativity you experience will dissolve.

"To strengthen your self-connection, you need to take ownership for your decisions, rather than waiting around for someone else to tell you what to do. Who else will do it for you? When it comes to your thriving, you truly do know best. Why not prompt yourself to begin?"

– *The Insightful Journey*

K

Kickstart

Launching Out of Procrastination

Procrastination wastes potential. Oftentimes we believe that we must wait for something or someone else to set us into action, when in reality, we develop our own strength and self-confidence when we take a simple step out of a stagnant period. With that being said – let's not wait to dive in.

My Prompts for a Kickstart

Where do I currently find myself on my independence journey – how good am I at motivating myself? To what extent do I wait for others to tell me what to do, rather than giving myself permission to do so?

Which area of my life do I currently need to give myself a kickstart in the most? If I do not know where to start, is there a prompt I could give myself to heal my balance in mind, body, or spirit?

When I am feeling balanced, it is likely that I am ready to give myself a prompt for moving on one of my goals. What is one small prompt that I can give myself to take action?

L

Laughter

Giving Yourself Permission to Laugh

Sometimes we easily surrender to humorous experiences with others; other times we hold back out of fear of judgement. Sometimes we are able to find the comical lightness in scrapes we encounter along the journey; other times we become too rigid with ourselves. It is always self-loving to yield to laughter in your relationships with others and with yourself, rather than trying to hold onto your 'serious adult' position. Laughter is infinitely cathartic and healing.

My Prompts for Laughter

What is one joyful memory I can think of where I could not stop laughing? Do I make enough time for these life-giving experiences in my life?

Do I resonate either with the idea of growing in a laughing relationship with myself, or being more vulnerable in a humorous way with others?

Is there anything I need to let go of so that I can give myself permission to laugh?

M
Miracles

More Miracles Than You Know

Rather than believing that miracles only arrive into our lives randomly, like winning the lottery, we can reframe our mindset to notice that miracles are prominent in everyday, seemingly mundane experiences. Training yourself to perceive miracles in your everyday experiences will allow you to be inspired by your life. To do so, you need to notice what is simply good and going well for you right now on your path. When we are busy or distracted, we can become wound up and forget to have gratitude for miracles such as the health of ourselves and our loved ones, what we have overcome and survived in life so far, and the blessing of being able to work towards thriving. It is well worth making this time to perceive the 'miracles of the now'.

My Prompts for Miracles

What have I survived through that amazes me? What have my loved ones, or the inspirational people that I look up to, survived through that amazes me?

When I look back on my journey, do I remember the landscapes of dreaming, mindful doing, and patience that were required for me to travel through so that I could become stronger? How are my past travels miraculous, and what can I learn from them now?

Is there something in my life that I have been taking for granted, like something kind that someone did for me this week or something I overcame? How can I have gratitude for these simple miracles (perhaps I could thank myself, or reach out to thank someone else)?

Layer Five: Engaging with Life Differently

When you engage with life differently, you will find yourself immersed in experiences that calm you, that draw out all of your inborn potential.

"We all live our lives in a linear state of growth in our bodies: being born, growing, and dying. Though within the years that encompass this greater development, we have the opportunity to be a part of many creations that we give birth to, nourish to growth, and complete."

– The Insightful Journey

N

New to the World Everyday

Out with the Old

Today is not just another ordinary day! We have more choice and autonomy to engage with ourselves, our experiences, and even our sense of place in life anew. In truth, it is only when we decide that this is not the case that we find ourselves becoming less self-loving and gentle with ourselves in life. Sometimes we cling to old narratives that we have made about ourselves, or even to our past experiences, to define who we are today. Your self-love journey is all about challenging the rusty beliefs that do not serve you, and contemplating how you can begin new chapters.

My Prompts for Being New to the World Everyday

Which ways of being new to myself, to my experiences, or to my sense of place speak to me right now?

What 'old stories' am I required to let myself outgrow so that I can welcome new chapters?

When I wake up tomorrow morning, what is one simple action I could take to engage with my life in an entirely new way, even if it is in a mundane area?

O

Open to Abundance

Where There Is Lack, There Is Abundant Potential

The beauty of being alive is that you have the capacity for what we call 'creation cycles'. When something in your life has ended, of course it is important to linger in those difficult feelings for some time so that you can process and heal. However, every ending is also a new beginning. The abundant harvests of our life are the times where we have plenty as a result of a journey of valleys and peaks that led to this larger view. We always plummet again, but when we are at the bottom, we are in a place of abundance because there is endless creative potential. Opening to abundance is about noticing that there are worlds within worlds both within yourself, and within the world at large.

My Prompts for Being Open to Abundance

How could I transition from thinking about my potential in terms of
limits, and instead reflect on in terms of abundance?

Am I growing towards the end point of a 'harvest' in my life right now, where all of the dreams that I am bearing will come to ultimate fruition?

How would it feel to be able to share with loved ones, or even with those less fortunate, through an experience of abundance?

P

Play

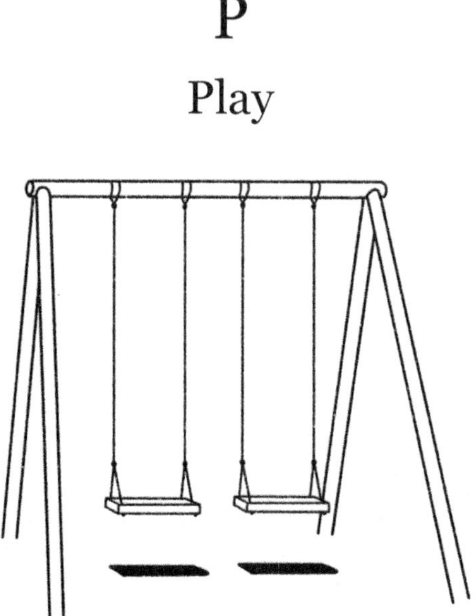

More Room for Play Than You Think

As we spoke of in Laughter, there is no need for us to hold onto the notion of what adulthood 'should' look like. We sometimes think we have to go about our lives in a particularly linear way, checking off an endless series of boxes – but play is about letting our 'inner child' support us through this process. We can integrate our inner child by making time for ourselves beyond our responsibilities, and also by letting our youthful spirit come through us when we feel its nudge. You can make efforts to no longer withhold your playful side by understanding the most mindful times and ways to express it.

My Prompts for Play

What did I like to do as a child?

What does my playful side look like now? How do I express it to those who I am comfortable with, or when I am alone?

Does playing around feel uncomfortable or unnecessary to me? If so, how could I step out of my comfort zone by surrendering to play for even five minutes this week?

Layer Six: Enhancing Mindfulness

When you enhance your mindfulness, you will come to know and love yourself better.

"You deserve to know yourself deeply, to be in conversation with yourself so that you can own your truths. When you illuminate all that lingers beneath the surface, you become aware of your life – from this awareness, you give yourself the next steps that you need to take."

– The Insightful Journey

Q

Quietness

Settling Into Stillness

Depending on your personality, you may or may not be familiar with the value of quietness. In this prompt, we invite you to notice what your belief about quietness is, and what you think you could do to integrate quietness into your life in a healthy way if you have not done so already. The benefit of settling down to be quiet and still with yourself is that you realise that this is what you need to replenish yourself – especially if you are someone who has a busy life. Rather than 'pushing through' and 'doing more', quietness is often the needed medicine.

My Prompts for Quietness

Am I more of an introvert or an extrovert? Do I naturally give myself quiet time to recharge, or do I let myself burnout by trying to keep up with the people and events in my life?

Why do I think that practising quietness would be valuable to my journey (e.g. allowing me to calm down, allowing me to be introspective)?

How could I make Quietness a safe place for me to land? Perhaps I could watch guided meditations or deep breathing videos, do yoga, listen to soft music, or simply sit and do nothing for five minutes. What speaks to me?

R
Reflection

What Currently Matters Beneath the Surface

Really, reflection is what you have been doing all along so far in this guide. Going a step further into quietness, you are looking into what is currently important to you in your life – which is your journey of balance and self-love. Reflections based on what is happening in your life at present are the most important, as these are what enable you to continue growing in the areas that matter most. Still, other 'currents' – of the past or future – can enter when you are settling into reflections on the present. Through this prompt, allow yourself to surrender and become attuned to the now.

My Prompts for Reflection

When was the last time I reflected on my life? Can I remember what I discovered about myself?

How could practising reflection support me as I work towards my goals and love myself? How often do I realistically have the time to reflect, and what medium works best for me?

Would I describe my life as rapid, slow, or counterproductive right now? Based on this awareness, what reflective conversation do I need to have with myself right now (e.g., if my life is fast-paced, I may need to take 10 minutes to renew my mind, body, and spirit balance)?

S

Signs to Follow

You Are Divinely Guided

Within you, you have a deep need to know whether you are being affirmed or resisted in your life – whether you are exactly where you are meant to be, or if it is time for a change. The Signs to Follow chapter is unique from the others as it invites you to look more closely for meaning in your external environments as it relates to animal encounters and patterns in natural landscapes. We are all being guided in this life; similarly to how we have to train ourselves to see 'miracles of the now', we can be more mindful when we are walking the High Road so that we unveil the meta-signs in our surroundings.

My Prompts for Signs to Follow

Have I ever witnessed a sign in my life? If so, do I remember the impact it had on my life at the time?

Is there a particular animal, element, or pattern in nature that has always resonated with me? If so, why?

Do I have time to invite myself for a walk today, this week, or this month for a 'meta-signs scavenger hunt' (preferably in nature)? During the walk, I can plan to be extra-attentive to my surroundings, and reflect here afterwards on what I found meaningful.

T

The Time is Now... Breathe

Catch Up with Your Breath

It is time to make time for you. To breathe and be with yourself, which you can do at best by being aware of the moments where you tend to feel stressed or distant from what is happening in front of you. Although we become accustomed to measuring time by the clock, 'moment o'clock' is the time that it truly always is. There is no feeling that is more life-affirming than knowing you are in the right place at the right time. Breathing where you are for a few minutes is often all you need to become immersed in the present moment to your fullest capacity.

My Prompts for The Time is Now... Breathe

How would I describe my relationship to the present moment? Are there times where I tend to drift, getting stuck in my head about the past, future, or even in my own problems?

What experiences cause me to feel like I am immersed in the present? If they are positive, how could I do them more often? If they keep me stuck in my comfort zone, how could I take action in that area and enjoy my time that way (e.g. if I am always present when watching movies, maybe I have been hiding my passion for scriptwriting or attending film festivals)?

Realistically, how much time could I make in a given week, or during a given day, to breathe or practise body awareness? What 'kickstart' could I give myself to do so (e.g. setting a visible reminder somewhere, taking two minutes during my lunch break, etc)?

Layer Seven: Connecting with Meaning

When you connect with meaning, you will feel a deep peace in knowing your place in this world.

"What is truly gold within you is the person that you are at your best, who you become when you choose to be interested in what you see flickering within, needing to expand."

– *The Insightful Journey*

U

Ultimate Calling

The Universe Is for You

You can have whatever you ask for – so long as it relates to the path of your ultimate calling. When you accept that you want to move into a fulfilling relationship with your authentic self, and expand on your true gifts as you progress in life, you will find yourself connecting to a universal energy. The greater good of everyone is involved when you care about your own greater good, so the universe is going to work in your favour – just not always the way that you expect it to. You will often have to do more work in the current phase of your calling, accepting more of yourself rather than less. However, you will also attract more onto your path, and feel so much better within yourself that there will be less resistance as you journey towards these dreams.

My Prompts for My Ultimate Calling

What am I 'calling up' to arrive on my path right now?

Do I have any ideas as to what the current phase of my ultimate calling might be? How do these future dreams feel to me – do I allow myself to melt into them often enough so that I can really immerse myself with where I am in my life and am headed?

Can I think of a time in my life where I felt disconnected from a sense of meaning or purpose? How could remembering my ultimate calling help me in situations like these?

V
Value

Creating Value in Life

You are the one who gets to decide what you hold to a high priority in your life. Although it can take time to ensure that you are living according to values that align with your authentic self, rather than values that you have absorbed from other people or trends, deciding this for yourself will make you feel that you are living a quality life. You will trust in yourself and your decisions more, because you will have a mindful guideline of what is of 'low-value' to your growth, and what is of 'high-value'.

My Prompts for Value

What do I surround myself with that creates forward momentum, builds my self-confidence, or offers me a sense of meaning and connection in the world? I can consider this to be 'high-value'.

Do I engage with the 'high-value' aspects that I brainstormed more often, or their opposite? This is likely 'low-value'. What changes would I like to focus on right now to enrich my life?

What is something that I have never done before but have always admired that could potentially add value to my life?

W
Withitness

A Big-Picture Outlook

Withitness relates to the ability to view life from a bird's eye view. It is about finding balanced meaning through understanding the dynamic between your subjective, individual life, and how it fits into an objective, collective well-being. When you are thriving at your best, you contribute to collective thriving, and vice versa. Understanding this perspective is important so that you can be humble, and feel empowered by the reality of life. Yes, there is work to do – but when you are doing it from the most foundational place of natural self-love, it helps everything in the world to 'work' together in harmony.

My Prompts for Withitness

What progress have I made on my journey so far in moving from 'within' to 'with-it'?

How often do I think about the greater picture, the meaning of life, or consider alternative perspectives? Do I limit myself to one worldview too often, and if so, how could I challenge myself to broaden the scope (e.g. affirming, researching, reflecting, etc)?

When I honestly reflect on my life, what are the areas that I currently feel stubborn, resistant, or even egoistic towards? How could I find new 'dimensions' of potential meaning to uncover, remembering that there is always more than what meets the eye?

X

X Marks Your Spot

Treasure Wherever You Go

This chapter is a reminder that everywhere you go, you carry your 'inner riches' with you. It is also somewhat of an existential reminder – not only is it self-loving to breathe life into what is within you, but it is also true that the consequence for not doing so is that you die with your dead dreams. Any moment in life is an opportunity for X to mark the spot; no matter how barren the path may appear to be, you know that there is more under the surface for you to tap into.

My Prompts for X Marks the Spot

Do I feel that I am on a path in life right now that is leading me to more places where X marks the spot?

Do I tend to think that I do not have enough externally (e.g. money, resources, connections) and use these factors as excuses to limit myself? How can I remind myself that only the bare basics are needed in the beginning, and trust that I already have all that I need within?

When I am struggling to stay in alignment with all I have learned about myself in my reflections, how can I remind myself that I will not die with my buried treasure within? Perhaps this can be a motivating, grounding force for me during times of turbulence.

Layer Eight: (Un)ending

When you remind yourself the journey is unending, you will be able to return to this guide whenever you are ready to start anew. We invite you to allow this ending to be your beginning, and to express gratitude to yourself for walking the High Road.

"Every day, you have the choice to build upwards. You know that each time you do this, you add a layer, an amendment to what was empty before. It is only human for there to be times where you want to turn back, though do you really believe you will ever stop wanting more for yourself out of self-love?"

– The Insightful Journey

Y

Yes to Life

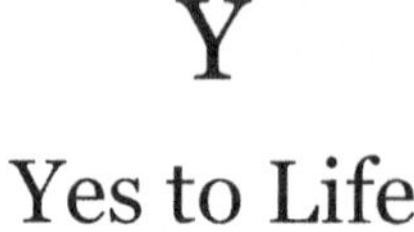

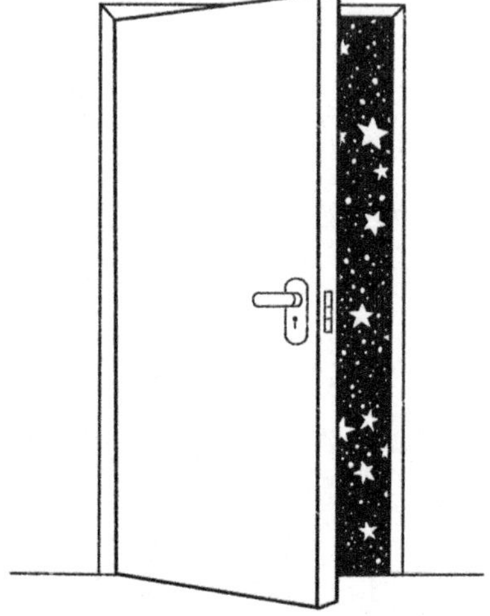

Yes to the Unknown

The times at which we most want to say no to life occur when the unknown is lurking behind the door we have put our hand on. We often take our hand away from the door and stay inside, saying no because we feel so unsure about ourselves. It is important for us to be brave and continue twisting the handle open. We often surprise ourselves by how much we are truly capable of when we allow ourselves to walk out of new doors – it is always life-affirming, for we gather the experiences we need to know and love ourselves better.

My Prompts for Saying Yes to Life

Is there anything in my life that I have judged without trying, shutting the door without stepping through? Next time this opportunity or one similar to it crosses my path, could I challenge myself to say yes, even if it scares me?

What is a new door that my mind began to ponder while reading *The Insightful Journey*, or while I was doing my inner work in this journal? How do I honestly feel about this newness? It is normal if I am afraid.

Remembering my Toolkit, how can I be gentle, kind, and loving with myself, working through my fear as I continue navigating experiences beyond my comfort zone?

Z

Zeroes Are No Longer Permitted

A Moment of Gratitude

Thank yourself for choosing to accept more of yourself. Thank yourself for choosing not to accept less of yourself. Thank yourself for beginning to build a foundation for your life. Thank yourself for caring about your own self-love. Thank yourself for caring to learn about what balanced efforts look like. Why? Because the High Road isn't easy to find, and yet you found it anyway. Not only did you find it, but the completed pages in this journal strongly show that you are walking it, growing into a better version of yourself one letter at a time.

My Prompts for Zeroes Are no Longer Permitted

What was the most rewarding for me to reflect on in this journal?

What am I most proud of myself for overcoming, outgrowing, or surrendering to through this inner work?

How am I going to lovingly, respectfully, and patiently hold myself accountable for returning to the High Road when unsteady terrain arises in the future? Although this book may be finished, my journey is unending. How can I make it my priority to commit to this truth?

Walking the High Road: An A-Z Guide is a series supported by and delivered through *Thrive: Enabling Potential.*

Thrive curates immersive experiences for those looking to expand their personal or professional development. Through literature, inspiring keynote speakers, engaging workshops, and retreats, our work has consistently enriched the lives of the individuals, teams, and educators who have engaged with us.

Our team is passionate about creating new and inspiring ways for you to thrive. If you are interested in being a part of what we offer, please do not hesitate to reach out to us on our website.

Let's work together to create an immersive experience for you or your team to enable your full potential.

www.enablingpotential.ca

Printed in Dunstable, United Kingdom